Quotations From
The Pulpit

Quotations From The Pulpit

Allen H. Lipis

January 2005

Preface

On January 1, 2003, I assumed the presidency of Congregation Beth Jacob in Atlanta, Georgia, the largest orthodox synagogue in Atlanta with about 560 families. Beth Jacob prides itself on being "the orthodox synagogue for all Jews," and it is. The synagogue has a broad range of religious observance, from very observant rabbis to those who drive to shul and do not keep kosher.

As president, one of my duties was to sit on the bimah during Friday night, Shabbos, and other holiday services to the right of the Torahs while the senior rabbi, Rabbi Ilan Feldman, sat to the left of the Torahs. At the end of the service, Rabbi Feldman would announce the various donations to the synagogue, the recent births, bar/bat mitzvahs and weddings that week within the membership, and other events that were to take place within the synagogue over the next few weeks. I would finish off the announcements by thanking the young man that was finishing the last few prayers during services, ask that any visitors to the synagogue that wished to have lunch with one of our families get in touch with Mr. Cohen, one of our members who saw to it that the visitor was connected with an appropriate family for lunch. In addition, I would speak about one aspect of the synagogue that related to the board of trustees, which usually related to financial matters. I then would finish my announcements with a quotation on some sort, since I am a great fan of quotations. In order to not end the announcement on a serious note related to money, the quotations were chosen to be funny, clever, insightful, or just brilliant.

As time went on, I would try to pick quotations that were related to the synagogue issues I was discussing, so that my announcement had a theme to it. And as I found the membership listening for these quotations, I increased the number of quotations if they were short and pithy from

only one to usually three, all on the same theme. After several months, members who did not hear the quotation would ask me to tell them what the quotation of the day was, as I was beginning to be known as the man with a quotation. I would be asked at the Kiddush, afterward as I walked home, and even the next day when I was out shopping. While I could not remember them all, I usually had a quotation handy and could give them something that would satisfy them.

I was asked on several occasions if I would send the quotations out by e-mail, since Beth Jacob had an e-mail notification network to announce recent events. I declined to do so, for I thought that it would be more useful to organize them all into a pamphlet after my term as president was up, so they would all be together in one place. That is the justification for this pamphlet.

The selection of these quotations was not easy. I had to satisfy a very religious audience that had just finished Shabbos morning prayers, so the quotations could not be nasty, sexy, hurtful, or silly. I spent about two hours per week picking out the three quotations that I selected, and that often required reading hundreds of quotations, narrowing down the list to a half dozen of them, then picking the final three and then deciding in what order to give them, often leaving the funniest of them for last.

I have decided to present the quotations in the chronological order that they were given, for there is no other order that seems more rational. I have removed the other parts of my announcements, for they do not fit with the objective of this pamphlet, which is to provide the quotations that the members looked forward to hearing each week for two years. However, I have included a part of the announcement that led up to the quotations where it was useful to set the tone for the quotations that followed.

For those of you that heard these quotations from the pulpit, you now have a record of what you heard. For those of you that missed them, I hope you get as much enjoyment out of reading them as I had in putting them together.

Finally, in order to provide a complete record of speeches I gave during my presidency, I thought I would include them in this pamphlet, for I think they add a certain degree of flavor to the content.

Allen Lipis
January 4, 2005

January 4, 2003

For those of you that don't know me, my name is Allen Lipis, and you have elected me to be your president this year. I want to thank you for the honor and privilege to serve this congregation. I will do my best to meet your expectations.

One thing I can say. I am not looking forward to being on this bimah because first I have to get here early, second I have to stay awake, and last I have to look like I know what I am doing. I may fail at all three.

I have been a member of this shul for thirty years, and some of you I count as my very good friends. With my wife, our Jewish observance grew here, my three children all grew up here, and now my grandchildren are growing up here. Even so, I know many of you only by your face, and we really haven't met; and still others I don't know at all.

I want to meet all of you, especially the people I don't know to discuss your vision for this synagogue and any other issue you want to talk about, so please introduce yourself to me when you get a chance.

If you are attending the luncheon today for the installation of the shul's officers, you will hear my vision for Beth Jacob. If you aren't coming, then I hope you will read it in the next BJ bulletin.

I want to try to inspire you each time I speak from this bimah with a wonderful quotation I find inspirational. Here is the first one from Michelangelo: "Trifles make perfection and perfection is no trifle."

January 4, 2003: BJ Inaugural Speech

In Pirkei Avot, there is a saying, "Keep three things in mind . . . : know where you came from, know where you are going, and know before whom you will have to give a strict account." Ultimately, we must all give a strict account to God, but as president of your synagogue, I start with the position that I must give a strict account to all of you as members of this congregation. I serve at your pleasure, and I hope to live up to your expectations, knowing that some of you may have conflicting expectations, and it will be impossible to please all of you all of the time. Just remember that I still am one of you, and I do have a full-time day job. I accepted this responsibility because I love this place, and I will do my very best to meet your needs and the shul's needs. Just have a little rachmanos on me!

Now where did we come from? We come from all walks of Judaism, some orthodox by birth, some with no knowledge of Judaism whatsoever, and many of us in between. Yet we all see that this shul is the real thing—no gimmicks, no shortcuts, no nonsense, but an honest, straightforward, adult guide to being intensely Jewish. We are the orthodox synagogue for all Jews with the emphasis on all. We pick our religious leadership with the objective of making us better Jews by inspiring us to grow Jewishly day by day, month by month, year by year so that we have come to understand the words of Emerson that "the years teach much which the days never know."

I want each of you to look back a year ago, or even five years ago if you were here then and ask how your life changed Jewishly. Hopefully, you will be able to recount the positive changes that have occurred in your life and give this shul some credit for helping you make those changes. One of the major objectives for my administration is to continue to provide the atmosphere that will allow each of you to grow at your own speed. Men will argue over religion—write for it, fight for it, die for it, anything but live for it (Walter Colton). In this shul, we are trying to live for it. That is what Congregation Beth Jacob is all about.

As I see my mission going forward, two critical issues must be addressed. The first and foremost issue is the financial stability of the synagogue. We cannot run a shul when we have to worry every month about paying our bills. While many Jewish organizations have deficits and do that as a normal form of existence, my expectation is to avoid a financial crisis. We have added excellent new staff. We have built magnificent Heritage Hall, expanded our chapel and kitchens, and renovated the early childhood classrooms. We are now finishing phase 2 by moving the administration upstairs into our old social hall, adding a new conference room, and creating a youth center where the old administration used to be. These additions will help to meet your needs and the shul's needs. I don't have to tell you that all this costs money.

The critical issue is not reducing costs but increasing revenue. In terms of the operating costs of this synagogue, the focus will be on fund-raising events, and we have many of them already underway. In January, we offer you our first eventless raffle. For $18 a ticket, you can win a $6,000 bond or two roundtrip tickets anywhere on Air Tran, or four other excellent prizes. In February we offer you the Southeast Kosher Festival, more than fifty exhibitors all in Heritage Hall displaying their kosher products. You will be able to see the latest in kosher items, taste the samples, meet the experts, and have a great time. Right on its heels we move on to our Purim Festival, with a different group of Jewish vendors and a major Purim Seudah. We expect to offer you real barbeque for your dining pleasure. In May, we will offer you the first ever Chinese Auction, the opportunity to win fifty or more substantial prizes. On the drawing boards are other possible fund-raisers: semimonthly kosher dinners in Heritage Hall created by esteemed chefs from the best restaurants in Atlanta, a golf tournament, casino night, an art auction, a Scotch tasting evening, a bricks at Beth Jacob with your name or the name of a loved one engraved on it, an expanded BJ directory, bingo in Heritage Hall, a concert series, a new Torah, and an annual Beth Jacob dinner. Not all these ideas are practical, and not all of them can be implemented during a single year; but we will focus on them and other ideas to raise funds not just from our congregation but drawing from all of Atlanta in order to meet the operating costs of the synagogue.

The honest fact is that dues constitute less than 50 percent of our expenses, and if we add to that all other religious fund-raisers such as the Kol Nidre appeal, Simchat Torah, High Holiday Honors, Aliyahs, sponsorships, cemetery fees, lockers and the rest, together they all add up to about two-thirds of the budgeted expenses. We need to raise $250,000 in nonreligious fund-raising events if we expect to maintain a balanced budget. One of the main duties of your board is to do that, and we need your support.

A few of you have already told us that the synagogue expects too much money from its members. Some of you may not be able to pay your dues or your rededication fund pledge or the Heritage Hall fees. We know you have other financial obligations, and we have always been accommodating. We have revised our dues structure. We have carefully evaluated facilities similar to Heritage Hall, and we believe our prices are fair and reasonable. We expect you to honor your rededication fund pledge to the best of your ability because we signed contracts with the architect, the construction company, and many other vendors based on these pledges. In short, we do not expect Beth Jacob to be at the bottom of your priority list. Be fair with us, and we will be fair with you. This synagogue has its own bills to pay, and it should not have to depend on only a few generous or wealthy families.

The second objective is to meet your religious, social, and educational needs. I know our religious services are outstanding, but I am sure our rabbi is always interested in how they can be improved.

Regarding Jewish education, the addition of the Kollel on our property, along with our rabbis, goes a long way in supporting your adult educational needs. Regarding social programs, we are and will be addressing the urgent needs of our teenagers, our singles, our young married couples, and those married with young children. These four groups are the future of our synagogue, and we must retain their support by offering them programs that meet their needs. The shul staff is already addressing these groups, but I want to explore how the board can do its part to make these groups feel important in this synagogue.

In short, I expect to focus your board of trustees on money and members, money and members, M&M. It's simple to say and hard to do. The critical ingredient in how well we succeed is you. You have the purse strings, and you have religious, educational, and social needs. My job, the board's job, this staff's job is to inspire you to greatness, to allow you to grow, to make you love this place because it continues to have a positive impact on your life.

Let me make this simple observation. Serving on the Board of Trustees of Congregation Beth Jacob is both an honor and a privilege. The thirty-one members of your board plus all past presidents do this because we all want to contribute in some small way to your growth as a Jew and to our own growth. We are doing this out of respect for our religion and for our commitment to our heritage. We pray that you will benefit greatly from our efforts, but I know that we who are involved will gain enormously by our participation. It has been my experience that the people who gain the most are the ones who are active, who are involved, who make and keep commitments and dare to do. Where do you think these expressions come from?

- "The more a man understands, the more is expected of him." (Chofetz Chaim)
- "The chief thing is not to study but to do."
- "A journey of ten thousand miles begins with the first step."
- "Genius is 1 percent inspiration and 99 percent perspiration." (Thomas Edison)
- "Fortune sides with him who dares."
- "An ugly patch is nicer than a beautiful hole."
- "It is better to have loved and lost than never to have loved at all."
- "Never in the field of human conflict was so much owed by so many to so few." (Winston Churchill)

Your board is a working board. I expect to deal with the critical issues facing this synagogue. I will begin by focusing on realistically balancing the budget, but I want to work on a strategic plan for the next ten years, something we have never done and really need. This will require some serious thinking about the future of this synagogue and how we are going to get there.

Let me conclude with a story from Joseph Telushkin's book Uncommon Sense.

> Rabbi Elzik, son of Rabbi Yekel, from Crakow, Poland, was very poor, but the rabbi had great faith in God. One night he dreamed that he should look for buried treasure in Prague, Czechoslovakia, over two hundred miles away, under a bridge that led to the king's palace. After dreaming the same dream for a third time, he set off for Prague. When he got to the bridge, it was guarded day and night, so he was afraid to start digging. Finally, the captain of the guards, having seen him day after day at the bridge, asked him what he was doing there. When Rabbi Elzik told the guard about his dream, the guard started laughing. The guard then told the rabbi that he too had a dream that he should go to Cracow and dig for treasure under the stove in the room of a Jew, a Jew named Elzik, the son of Yekel—that was his name! And he laughed again.

Rabbi Elzik bowed, traveled back home, and dug up the treasure under his stove.

Take this story to heart. The treasure is right here, in your home, in your family and friends, and in this synagogue. The place where this treasure can be found is the place on which I stand and place where you now sit.

Jan 11, 2003

My quote for this Shabbos is,

"If things aren't the way you like them, like them the way they are."

January 18

My quote for this Shabbos is apropos of the faith Nachshon ben Aminadav had in being the first to walk into the Red Sea up to his neck:

"With faith there are no questions; without faith there are no answers."

January 25

The quote this week is a wonderful line from Sam Levenson:

"Insanity is hereditary; you get it from your children."

February 1

A quote from the Talmud:

"Three things in human life are important. The first is to be kind. The second is to be kind. And the third is to be kind. The beginning and end of Torah is performing acts of loving-kindness."

February 8

We have a board of thirty-one members, all committed to the financial stability of this synagogue. We have seventy-five committees actively working in this synagogue—from ushers, to security, to educating our children, to religious activities, to sisterhood, the men's club, and the Mikvah Association.

Why do we do this? It is because we believe in this shul and in its mission. So here is the quote for today from William P. Morris:

"Respectable men and women content with the good and easy living are missing some of the most important things in life. Unless you give yourself to some great cause, you haven't even begun to live."

February 15

You will receive a letter from me shortly regarding the Yizkor book. The Yizkor book is designed to honor or remember a loved one. This year we want to print a short story about the people you wish to remember. Please consider writing a short paragraph about a person so we can keep his or her memory alive. It will do much to enhance your life and ours. The Yizkor book suggests the quote from Horace Rutledge for today:

"When you look at the world in a narrow way, how narrow it seems! When you look at it in a mean way, how mean it is! When you look at it selfishly, how selfish it is! But when you look at it in a broad, generous, friendly, spirit, what wonderful people you find in it."

February 22

That brings me to the quote this week, which reflects the simple idea that if you think you can or if you think you can't, you're probably right. The quote is as follows:

"There's no thrill in easy sailing when the skies are clear and blue, there's no joy in merely doing things which any one can do.

But there is some satisfaction that is mighty sweet to take, when you reach a destination that you thought you'd never make."

March 1

As you all know, the SE Kosher Festival last Sunday was a spectacular success. Heritage Hall sold out with eighty-five exhibitors; over 2,200 people attended the festival. Over one hundred volunteers from Beth Jacob supported this event, one of the largest events in Beth Jacob's history and certainly one of the most successful. From the beginning, the festival committee worried whether they would sell exhibit space, whether they would get a strong attendance, whether they would run out of food, and whether they could muster enough volunteers. They worried so much that they succeeded. If one phrase could sum it up, it is that they had the will to succeed and the professionalism to make the vendors, the public, and the volunteers proud to be associated with this event. If you were in any way associated with the SE Kosher Festival, would you do me the honor to raise your hand now so everyone can see who you are.

That leads me to the quote for the day, a lovely poem called "The Man Who Thinks He Can" by Walter Wintle:

> If you think you are beaten, you are;
> If you think you dare not, you don't;
> If you'd like to win, but think you can't,
> It's almost a cinch you won't.
> If you think you'll lose, you're lost,
> For out in the world we find
> Success begins with a fellow's will;
> It's all in the state of mind.
>
> If you think you're outclassed, you are;
> You've got to think high to rise.
> You've got to be sure of yourself before
> You can ever win a prize.
> Life's battles don't always go
> To the stronger or faster man;

But soon or late the man who wins
Is the man who thinks he can.

The women who made this happen thought they could, refused to yield, and conquered every worry they had. Yasher Koach.

March 8

Because many of you want to know what is really going on in the shul, I want to inform you of a few errors in the recently mailed Jacob's Vice, it usually is Jacob's Voice, for the month of Adar and for Purim. Perhaps, you missed the purple insert section, so let me summarize it for you. Sybil says in her article that we now have reclining loungers with a massage, a bartender to serve you any drink you desire, a gourmet chef on call 24/6, a tanning bed facility, indoor tennis courts, a music room for tap dancing and ballet, a hair salon, a workout gym, and self-help videos for the maintenance staff.

Rebecca adds that the swimming pool at Beth Jacob is Olympic size, that we now bus our preschool children using a surplus bus from Puerto Rico, serve a hot breakfast to the children daily, and we will soon have two teachers for every child in our preschool. Rabbi Avi maintains that his davening will bring success to the Braves and Hawks, as it did for the Rams when he lived in St. Louis.

And finally, Avraham Litzman announced that the shul will be offering the new Heritage Hall High Stakes Bingo, and Rabbi Ilan will assume responsibility for operations. In addition, nonelectric, mechanical slot machines will be installed on the back of your pew seats so you can play during the repetition of the Amidah, the rabbi's sermon and Kiddush.

The error that must be pointed out is that the massage chair, the bartender, the gourmet chef, the tanning facility, the music room, the hair salon, the gym, and the Olympic swimming pool are only, and I mean only, available to the staff and the board of trustees. I am very, very sorry. In addition, Rabbi Avi is also praying for the success of our High Stakes Bingo; I am sure he would welcome your prayers. Finally, if a slot machine is not available on the back of your pew soon, please let Avraham know. And if two teachers are not working exclusively with your child, kindly inform us.

Rabbi Lapin, last night said he would address the question of whether God wants us to be rich. That led me to the quotes for the day, which are from Woody Allen, because I feel just like him:

He said, "If only God would give me some clear sign, like making a large deposit in my name at a Swiss bank."

And he also said, "I don't want to achieve immortality through my work. I want to achieve it through not dying."

By the way, if you are interested, please ask Sybil for a tour of the pool; Avraham also will be happy to show you the new pew slot machines.

March 15

The quote for today fits a bar mitzvah. It is this: "If a mother gives her children one gift, let it be passion. And the most important thing a father can do for his children is to love their mother."

March 22

The quote for today is a way of defining what the fear of God means. Robert Frost, the laureate poet, said it this way:

"The fear of God is that we shall not prove worthy in the eyes of someone who knows us at least as well as we know ourselves."

April 12

The quote for today is by Mother Teresa:

"People are often unreasonable and self-centered. Forgive them anyway.

If you are kind, people may accuse you of ulterior motives. Be kind anyway.

If you are honest, people may cheat you. Be honest anyway.

If you find happiness, people may be jealous. Be happy anyway.

The good you do today may be forgotten tomorrow. Do good today.

Give the world the best you have, and it may never be enough.
Give your best anyway.
For you see, in the end it is between you and God.
It never was between you and them anyway."

April 17: First Day of Pesach

The rabbi made the statement that since I had quoted Mother Teresa, members of the congregation had suggested to him that perhaps I was running out of quotes. He meant it in jest, of course. He went on say that I might even quote the Pope. Therefore, in order to guarantee that I would have sufficient quotes to give, he presented me with a new edition of Pirkei Avos, the Ethics of the Fathers, which is nothing but quotable quotes.

I then got up and said that it was funny that he should bring that subject up, because I had a quote from Pirkei Avos for today. The quote is as follows:

"A person of forbearance and patience excels over a hero, and any person who controls his or her emotions is better than the conqueror of a city." This quote is particularly appropriate given that we are the conquering country over Iraq.

From Samson Raphael Hirsch: "It follows that this task of self-control is an obvious one; and yet it is rated at being so difficult that a person who succeeds in it deserves far more praise and fame than the conquering hero of a city."

April 18: Second Day of Pesach

There is a prayer that is only said on festivals that occur on weekdays, so this prayer is not said often, even though it is such a powerful request. The prayer is this:

"Master of the universe, remember me for long life, for good life and for peace, good livelihood and sustenance, bread to eat, clothes to wear, wealth, honor, a long life engaged in Your Torah and Your commandments; and intelligence and insight to understand and discern the depths of Your mysteries. Grant a complete recovery to all our suffering and bless all our handiwork. Decree upon us good decrees, salvations and consolations. Nullify all harsh and evil decrees against us and dispose the feelings of the government, its counselors and ministers upon us for good. Amen."

If you cannot remember this long prayer, the shortened version is this: "God will provide—if only God will provide until He provides."

April 19

Two days ago, the rabbi suggested that I had so few quotes left that I might even have to quote the Pope.

Well, today I do have a quote from A. Pope, and it goes like this:

"He who serves his brother best—gets nearer God than all the rest."

And just to be absolutely clear, Rabbi, the quotation is from A. Pope, Alexander Pope, a well-known English poet who lived three hundred years ago, who wrote highly polished verse.

He also wrote,

"Teach me to feel another's woe,
To hide the fault I see.
That mercy I to others show,
That mercy show to me."

April 24

A few people have asked me to include Jewish quotations in my Shabbos announcements. Here are a few quotes from well-known secular Jews:

From Dorothy Parker, the writer: "If you want to know what God thinks of money, just look at the people he gave it to."

From André Maurois, the French biographer: "A successful marriage is an edifice that must be rebuilt every day."

From Groucho Marx: "I find television very educational. Every time someone switches it on I go into another room and read a good book."

May 3

I'm in a good mood, so here is the quote from Michael Pritchard for today: "You don't stop laughing because you grow old; you grow old because you stop laughing." Let me put it quite simply, "Laugh and the world laughs with you; snore and you sleep alone."

May 10

Tomorrow is Mother's Day. If your mother is still alive, I urge you to show your appreciation. If you are married, whether you have children or not, my advice is to treat your wife as well as you would treat your own mother. With that in mind, here are a few quotes about mothers:

From Robert Frost: "A diplomat is a man who always remembers a woman's birthday but never remembers her age."

From Carl Sandburg: "A baby is God's opinion that the world should go on."

"Cleaning your house while your kids are still growing is like shoveling the driveway before it has stopped snowing."

"Mothers of teens know why some animals eat their young."

From Cyrano De Bergerac: "A kiss is a rosy dot over the 'i' of loving."

"You can fool some of the people all of the time and all of the people some of the time, but you can never fool mom."

May 17

The quote for today comes from Rabbi Norman Schloss:

"Yesterday is history, tomorrow is a mystery. Today is a gift from God, that is why it is called the present."

That quote reminds me of the famous quote from W. C. Gannett:

"I expect to pass through life but once. If there is any kindness, or any good thing I can do to my fellow beings, let me do it now. I shall pass this way but once."

May 24

We will announce shortly a new program to raise $200,000 for the operation of the synagogue. Without your support, we will be in trouble. Only you know how important Beth Jacob is to you and your family. For me, it is an essential part of my life. Your presence here tells me that you must feel the same.

That leads me to the quotes for today, all of which focus on the difference between getting and giving.

William Arthur Ward said, "The momentary thrill of getting rarely equals the lasting joy of giving."

Winston Churchill said, "We make a living by what we get, but we make a life by what we give."

And finally George Foster summed it up this way: "What you are is God's gift to you and what you do with what you are is your gift to God."

May 27: Shavuos

The Torah has molded our character, regulated our behavior, and shaped our destiny. As Sa'adiah has said, "Our people is a people only by virtue of our possession of the Torah."

Regarding Shavuos, there is a this story by Rabbi Stephen Wise who at a public banquet happened to sit next to a lady who tried to impress him. She claimed that one of her ancestors witnessed the signing of the Declaration of Independence. Rabbi Wise could not resist replying, "My ancestors were present at the giving of the Ten Commandments."

May 31

In consideration of the upcoming marriage of our son, I present several quotes regarding the mitzvah of Shalom Bayis (marital peace or peace in your home).

The sages say, "An angry man is left with nothing but his anger." That's why an angry man is a fool.

Completing the thought, the Vilna Gaon said, "Attempting to stop an argument by arguing is the same as trying to wash your face in your own filth; the more you wash, the more you sully yourself."

On a more positive note, Rabbi Aharon Feldman says, "A woman's most deep-seated need is her need to be loved, admired and respected . . . . The most basic way to show respect to a wife is to pay attention to her when she speaks." In short, "the obligation on the husband is to make his wife happy."

And finally, Rav Eliyahu Dessler notes a remarkable truth of the difference between giving and getting: "We tend to love those to whom we give more than those from whom we receive."

June 7: Shavuos

Because we celebrate Shavuos today, I thought it would be appropriate to share several quotes related to the Torah:

The first quote is about prayer, and perhaps it will change your approach to it:

"When I pray, I pray swiftly because I am talking to God. When I study, I read slowly because God is talking to me."

B. C. Forbes made the comment that "the man without religion is like a ship without a rudder."

Immanuel Kant made this statement: "Two things profoundly impress me: The starry heavens above me and the moral law within me."

And finally, what do you call a Torah with a seat belt?

A Safer Torah!

June 14

This coming Monday, my wife and I leave to celebrate the marriage of our son. The rabbi just announced the engagement of his son, so we both have marriage on our minds. In anticipation of our sons' marriages, I thought that I would share some quotations on marriage with you.

First, "You don't marry someone you can live with—you marry the person who you cannot live without."

Mignon Mclaughlin said, "A successful marriage requires falling in love many times, always with the same person."

Ogden Nash said,
"To keep your marriage brimming,
With love in the loving cup,
Whenever you're wrong admit it;
Whenever you're right shut up."

A husband's last words should always be "OK buy it."

My favorite is what Simone Signoret said, "Chains do not hold a marriage together. It is threads, hundreds of tiny threads which sew people together through the years—more than passion or even sex!"

July 5

My perspective about our synagogue is that we have strong leadership; we have plenty of ideas, almost too many ideas. We have great minds and great ideas. What we need are strong managers, self-starter managers who can take an idea and make it happen. We need people who can organize, plan, and implement. If you are one of those people, please come talk to me. This shul needs your help.

With regard to managers who will aggressively implement, I offer the following quotations:

From Beverly Sills: "You may be disappointed if you fail, but you are doomed if you don't try."

From Judah HaNasi: "Action takes precedence over study."

From Justice Arthur Goldberger: "If Columbus had an advisory committee he would probably still be at the dock."

From Aristotle: "Well begun is half done."

From General George Patton: "Never tell people how to do things. Tell them what to do and they will surprise you with their ingenuity."

From Benjamin Jowett: "The way to get things done is not to mind who gets the credit for doing them."

July 12

Having spent a great deal of time recently with all my children and grandchildren and hearing so many announcements of children being born to our members, my quotes today deal with children.

Rabelais said, "A child is not a vase to be filled but a fire to be lit."

Joseph Joubert said, "Children have more need for models than critics."

Harold Hulbert said, "Children need love, especially when they do not deserve it."

Denis Waitley said, "The two greatest gifts you can give your children are the roots of responsibility and the wings of independence."

With regard to eating, Fran Lebowitz said it quite clearly, "Ask your child what he wants for dinner only when he is buying."

And the last quote is this: "Remember, growing older is mandatory; growing up is—optional." That's right, growing up is optional.

July 19

We sincerely and honestly need your help. We are up to big things. Please help us become an even greater place than we are today.

Please don't tell me you don't have the time. We can do a lot together, and we only need a little of your time. Together we can accomplish much in a short period of time. This week I saw a wonderful show in town called Thoroughly Modern Millie. It has at its core three young people who very much want to change their lives. They want the freedom and luxury of self-invention, something that is very American. I leave you with one quote from the musical, a great line that sums up my thoughts succinctly:

"You can make big changes in a week. Read the Bible."

August 9

My quote today is from Herbert Lehman, a governor of New York and then a US senator from New York. In a wonderful book called This I Believe, edited by Edward R. Morrow, Mr. Lehman wrote,

"Commonplace as it may sound, I am convinced that what we get out of life is in direct proportion to what we put into it . . . . Life is not a one-way street. What I do, what I say even what I think, inevitably has a direct effect on my relationship with others . . . [to] the degree that my attitude toward others has given proof of [my] loyalty, sincerity, honesty, courtesy and fairness, I have encouraged in others the same attitude towards me. Respect begets respect, suspicion begets suspicion, hate begets hate. It has been well said that 'the only way to have a friend is to be a friend.'"

August 16

William Arthur Ward said,
"Flatter me, and I may not believe you.
Criticize me, and I may not like you.
Ignore me, and I may not forgive you.
Encourage me, and I may not forget you."

I don't want to flatter, criticize, or ignore you. What I want is to encourage you to take on a significant role in this great synagogue. The reason is so that you will never forget what our mission is. It is more than merely davening. This shul has provided the leadership for Orthodox Judaism in Atlanta for the past fifty years and God willing for another fifty more. The Sanhedrin makes the following statement:

"You have three names:
The one you inherited,
The one your parents gave you,
And the one you make for your self."

For the names that people say about Congregation Beth Jacob, we, all of us, are always responsible, whether what we do is intentional or inadvertent, whether we are asleep or awake. The Sanhedrin says that "all men are responsible for one another." It is even more so for this institution that continues to give so much to all of you.

August 23

As president, my job is to help fill a number of volunteer positions. I am letting you all know from the pulpit in the hope that at least one of you will volunteer without me having to ask. Please see me or call me if you want to volunteer for one of these important assignments or even if you wish to suggest a name to me. All reasonable offers will be accepted.

Today's quote deals with volunteering and is adapted from Rashi:

"Naked a man comes into the world, and naked he leaves it; after all his toil, he carries away nothing—except the deeds he leaves behind."

August 30

Rabbi Feldman is in Israel this week for his grandson's bris, and he will be away next weekend for his son's aufruf and wedding in New Jersey. In honor of the rabbi's simchas, I present the following quotes:

For a newborn, Carl Sandburg said, "A baby is God's opinion that the world should go on."

For marriage, Randolph Ray said, "I would like to have engraved inside every wedding band [the words] Be kind to one another. This is the Golden Rule of marriage and the secret of making love last through the years."

September 7

I thought I would provide a couple of quotes related to education:

Robert Maynard Hutchins, the president of the University of Chicago and the man that introduced the study of the Great Books, said,

"The object of education is to prepare the young to educate themselves throughout their lives."

Learning is the best of all wealth; it is easy to carry, thieves cannot steal it, and tyrants cannot seize it; neither fire nor water can destroy it; and far from decreasing, it increases by giving.

I know that an education is expensive, especially a Jewish education, but the only thing more expensive than education is ignorance.

September 14

The quotes for today deal with love:

From Elbert Hubbard: "Love grows by giving. The love we give away we keep. The only way to retain love is to give it away."

From Henry Drummond: "You will find as you look back on your life that the moments that stand out, the moments when you have really lived are the moments when you have done things in a spirit of love."

From Les Miserables: "When you love another person, you are seeing the face of God."

September 27: Rosh Hashanah

The rabbis encourage all of us to observe Rosh Hashanah in a spirit of optimism, confident that God will accept our repentance and extend our lives. With that in mind, I want to paraphrase a few statements made regarding repentance from Gateway to Happiness by Rabbi Zelig Pliskin:

1. When you repent for what you have done wrong in the past, you should look at yourself as a newly created person and therefore your past wrongs are not identified with you . . . . You should look at yourself as if you were born on this day . . . In your eyes this day should be considered the beginning of your deeds as a new person.

2. By looking at your life as if you are starting from this present moment, you will free yourself from the heavy burden that is holding you back . . . . The heavy burden you carry on your shoulders for the past wrongs you did may vanish, because you now can look at your life as if everything were starting from tonight, from this New Year, from this new beginning.

3. If you do this, you will then feel encouraged to work on your own improvement.

October 4: Shabbos Shuvah

To repent for a wrong you committed, the rabbis say that you must take three steps:

1. Admit the sin.
2. Have regret for the wrong you did in the past.
3. Resolve to avoid doing that sin in the future.

You are asking for forgiveness by changing your attitude and even your actions. The essentials of teshuvah are the abandonment of the sin, spoken confession with a broken heart, and wholehearted regret.

Here are my quotes about forgiveness:

From Publilius Syrus: "How unhappy is he who cannot forgive himself."

From Dolores Huerta: "If you haven't forgiven yourself something, how can you forgive others?"

From Gerald Jampolsky: "I can have peace of mind only when I forgive rather than judge."

From Alexander Pope: "To err is human, to forgive, divine."

Putting all the quotes together, we get the following:

*   First, since God forgives, I should also forgive.
*   Next, to forgive, I should forgive myself first; then I will learn to forgive others.
*   Finally, only when I forgive myself and others can I hope to have peace of mind.

October 6: Kol Nidre

Ask me why I invest my money and I will tell you it is because I want to make money. Ask me why I work and I will tell you it is because I need to make money. But ask me why I work for Congregation Beth Jacob and I will tell you it is because we are building a great synagogue. Like each and every president before me, I work for this shul because of the love we have for what it stands for, the respect we have for the rabbis that serve it, and the devotion we have to Judaism.

Ask yourself one and only one question: how important is this synagogue to you? If the answer to that question is that this shul is important to you for your heart, for your mind, or for your soul, then make your donation tonight really matter. Yes, we have bills to pay, and dues only count for less than half of our budget, but more important we have a mission to be the orthodox synagogue for you and for your family.

If you love this place, and I know you do; if you believe in our mission, and I know you do; if you wish to serve others and I know you do, then make this moment count for yourself and for Beth Jacob.

Please push down the Kol Nidre donation card in your possession, put it in the envelope, and hand it in to an usher collecting them.

October 11: Succos

I am pleased to tell you that the Kol Nidre appeal last week by our rabbi was successful and met our expectations, in spite of the weak economy. I want to thank all of you for your generous support of our synagogue. For those of you who did not make a pledge, there is still time to do it now. The big problem is not the haves and have-nots—it's the give-nots. Bob Hope said, "If you don't have charity in your heart, then you have the worst kind of heart trouble."

We are approaching the time when the nominating committee for the board of trustees prepares a slate of officers and board members for next year. If you are interested in serving on our board of trustees, then please let me or the rabbi know so we can provide that information to the nominating committee.

With service to others in mind, the quote for today is a paraphrase from Charles Lamb:

The only true time you can call your own are the days that you devote to yourself. The days you serve other people should not count in measuring how old you are, for those days are other people's time, not your own. Therefore, take the number of years you have lived and deduct from that the days you have served other people. The more you serve others, the younger you really are, and the more you will find that you are still a young person.

October 12

Your board of trustees has agreed to pay to maintain the property around our synagogue so we expect to implement a beautiful, professionally designed landscaping plan. The start of that plan was implemented just outside the entrance to Heritage Hall. The rest will be implemented shortly. I think you will be impressed with the new and improved look of our property.

None of this has come easily, and we still have unfinished business. Anna Pavlova, the great Russian ballerina said, "Success depends in a very large measure upon individual initiative and exertion, and cannot be achieved except by dint of hard work." Vidal Sassoon says, "The only place where success comes before work is in a dictionary."

A reporter asked a bank president,

"Sir, what is the secret of your success?

"Two words"

"And, sir, what are they?"

"Right decisions."

"And how do you make the right decisions?"

"One word."

"And, sir, what is that?"

"Experience."

"And how do you get experience?"

"Two words"

"And, sir, what are they?"

"Wrong decisions."

November 1

Two weeks ago on Shemini Atzeret, the season of our rejoicing, I did not make any announcement, but I was prepared then to read a couple of quotes related to happiness. Unwilling to let them go to waste, here they are:

From Dale Carnegie: "Remember happiness doesn't depend upon who you are or what you have; it depends solely upon what you think."

From Albert Schweitzer: "Happiness? That's nothing more than good health and a poor memory."

"Happiness is like a kiss—in order to get any good out of it you have to give it to somebody else." (Unknown)

November 8

Here are a few cute sayings that I like.

The fellow who thinks himself a wit is usually half-right.

Doctors have discovered that hay fever can be either positive or negative. Sometimes the eyes have it and sometimes the nose.

Here's a poem called the "Tin Whistle."

> I bought a wooden whistle,
> But it wooden whistle,
> So I bought a steel whistle,
> But steel it wooden whistle,
> So I bought a lead whistle.
> Still it wooden lead me whistle,
> So I bought a tin whistle,
> And now I tin whistle.

November 15

In Judaism, many things come in threes. In general, it is a wonderful writing style, and it makes for easy listening. Here are just a few quotes that come in threes:

From the Talmud: "Three things spoil a man's health: worry, travel and sin."

From Judah HaNasi: "I have learned much from my teachers, more from my colleagues, but most from my students."

From Ethics of the Fathers: "Keep three things in mind and you will escape the results of evil: know where you came from, where you are going, and before whom you will have to give a full account."

From Israel Salanter: "Three things can be learned from a railroad: if you are one minute late, you miss it; the slightest deflection from the rails leads to disaster; and a passenger without a ticket may expect punishment."

Yiddish saying: "Give your ear to all, your hands to friends, but your lips only to your wife."

November 22

If you don't volunteer to help this shul, let me tell you what you risk. We can't support the police when we don't have the money. How important are the police outside this building to your security? You may make the decision nondebatable if we don't have the money. We can't support the SKIP program for your children without money. How important is that program for your children? We may not be able to continue the ECD program as it presently is, or maintain the staff we presently have without the money. In our budget, we do not have any fat to cut; your shul staff is efficient, and cutting cost will never solve our financial problem. The only solution is to increase our revenue. It's that simple.

If you have never been asked to volunteer, then I am asking you now. I'm asking each and every one of you to help. I need your help, and I need it now. I don't sit in your shoes, and I will not second-guess your reasons. Nor will I criticize you for your decision. I will just say this for myself. I run my own company, and I have major commitments to my company to make it successful. That is a full-time job. And yet I have found the time to be your shul president this year. President of BJ is a very demanding job, as demanding as running my own company. I am working here even though this synagogue demands a lot of my time and energy. With your support I'll give it my best for another year if you will have me.

If you are on reduced dues, then you owe us your time; if you come to shul on a regular basis, then you owe us your time; if you have children in one of our programs, if you attend lectures by our rabbis, if you attend programs we put on, if you pray here often, then you owe us your time. In short, if you use this place beyond coming for the high holidays, then you owe us your time.

You have only two choices; either you make a commitment of your time for fund-raising or donate your money to one of the outstanding orthodox synagogues in the world, this synagogue, or we cut back on services for you and your family. We either grow or decay, and that means you either help us with your time and your money or you force this great synagogue to decline. This is not a request; it is a forecast that is a virtual certainty. We cannot stay where we are today.

In line with this straight talk, I give you the following quotes:

From Rabbi Nachman of Bratslav: "If you do not help a person with trouble, it is as though you have brought trouble to him."

From the Vilna Gaon: "Only things acquired by hard labor and great struggle are of any value."

November 29

I am sorry I cannot be with you this shabbos as I am celebrating a wedding in Seattle. Last week, I made an impassioned plea for volunteers for the Southeast Kosher Festival. The result from that plea was an enormous outpouring of overwhelming, positive support from a variety of people volunteering their time to the Southeast Kosher Festival. In total, thirty people came forward within twenty-four hours and agreed to undertake assignments for the Kosher Festival, most of them to sell vendor booths for the Kosher Festival. Some immediately met me right after services before I could leave the pulpit, many cornered me at Kiddush, some called me at home, and many added themselves to the list at the Torah Day School brunch last Sunday. Thirty people volunteering for the Kosher Festival within a twenty-four-hour period tells me what a fantastic group of people we have in this congregation. While some of these people volunteer regularly for the shul, others were inspired to volunteer for the first time. Please note that there is still room for anyone wishing to volunteer. There is a lot to do, and we can use your help.

If I offended any of you for my tone or my directness, I do apologize. For those of you who came forward, my humble thanks. This is an amazing place, full of people who care deeply for each other and for what Beth

Jacob stands for. With the quality people we have, there is no limit to what we can accomplish.

December 6

Today's quotes deal with action, with execution, the single greatest factor in whether we succeed or fail:.

From A. Favre: "It is only those who never do anything who never make mistakes."

From James B. Conant: "Behold the turtle. He only makes progress when he sticks his neck out."

From Paul Valéry: "The best way to make your dreams come true is to wake up."

December 13

With the future of the shul on my mind, here are quotes related to the future:

Robert Kennedy is often associated with this quote, but it rightly belongs to George Bernard Shaw. He said, "You see things and you say, 'Why?' But I dream things that never were, and I say, 'Why not?'"

This is the cadet maxim at the US Military Academy at West Point:

"Risk more than others think is safe. Care more than others think is wise. Dream more than others think is practical. Expect more than others think is possible."

Finally there is this quote from Sophie Tucker, a famous American singer that my mother loved:

"I have been poor and I have been rich. Rich is better."

State of the Synagogue: 2004

I am honored to begin my second term as your president. I am also scared to assume this responsibility because I know the amount of effort it will take. There is a great deal of unfinished business at Congregation Beth Jacob, and I can only hope that I have the time, the ability, and the passion to meet your expectations.

I want to briefly summarize where the shul is today, what we did accomplish in 2003, then discuss what I hope to accomplish in 2004 and then take a few questions or comments from you.

In terms of the net assets of Congregation Beth Jacob, a year ago our assessment was the Beth Jacob was worth about $6 million after deducting our liabilities from the value of our land, building, and property. However, none of it is liquid.

The rededication fund had pledges of $4.1 million, but we estimate that over $300,000 is uncollectible, and considering our costs, we need to raise $270,000 more to come out even. We have enough cash to cover us for the next two years, however.

In 2003, the $1 million budget that I began the year with had a $150,000 deficit. I estimate that we will end the year with a deficit of $120,000, which is not good, but better than I expected. Every fund-raiser made money, SEKF, Purim, Raffle Annual Dinner, Annual Directory, and Heritage Hall but wasn't enough to cover our costs. We have had to draw upon our Wachovia line of credit, and we owe the bank about $300,000 on that line of credit, which is different from the rededication fund loan.

For 2004, we need to focus on major fund-raisers and finding lay people who want to manage fund-raising projects and market them beyond the BJ community. The major fund-raisers are SEKF, Annual Dinner/Directory, Casino Night/Raffle, Yizkor Book, and a new $25,000 fund-raiser yet undefined.

We will also launch the Malachim Society for upscale families to cover part of the operations of the shul. We will announce the program shortly. We have budgeted to raise at least $100,000 from Malachim Society membership.

We also need to launch a marketing program for Heritage Hall, review the ECD budget, and consider whether we need to raise the membership dues.

Shabbos Services produces two hundred people every week, three hundred plus for a bar/bat mitzvah, and four hundred of high holidays. Plus we run several other minyans. Our Shabbos bulletin announced forty-eight marriages in 2003, not all held at BJ, twelve bar/bat mitzvahs, and seventy-six births, many outside of Atlanta. Rabbi Ilan gave nineteen lectures besides his sermon and Rabbi Avi gave nine lectures and one ongoing class on Pirkei Avos. We had eighteen visiting rabbis who spoke to our shul throughout the year and five exceptional rabbis—R. Fleer, R. Emmanuel Feldman, R. Lapin, R. Benjamin Elon, a member of the Israeli Cabinet, and R. Berel Wein. There were twelve lectures by women, many of them rebbetzin. The Soapbox Lecture after Kiddush was a huge success with ten lay lectures in addition to the rabbis I just mentioned.

From an administrative perspective:

1. We moved into our new offices, after storing much of the office off-site.
2. We began in-house catering with a group of wonderful volunteers, making an average 50 percent profit on each event. Today's Kiddush was handled in-house by our volunteers.
3. Volunteers also prepared Kiddushes that were not sponsored so we don't have to pay an outside caterer.
4. We installed a new computer system called Chaverware, which tracks individual membership accounts, and that is linked to Peachtree Software, our accounting system for bill payment and budgeting.
5. We are updating all our membership and yahrzeit records.

But perhaps the highlight of the year was Rabbi Ilan's visit with Pres. George Bush. With less than two dozen rabbis invited to the White House, about two hundred of us listened to the rabbi after Kiddush as our rabbi recounted his visit. We hung on his every word for close to an hour about his trip, just as Rabbi Ilan listened intently to everything President Bush said. It was an exciting event for all of us.

During 2004, we had a substantial number of children programs, NCSY programs, singles programs, young couples programs, senior programs, sisterhood programs, and men's club programs. And after all that, we had eighteen other general programs, such as Friday night empty nestor dinners, Succos block party, and Shlock Rock concert, to name a few.

The most important issues your board will address this year are the following:

1. Strategic Plan
2. Focus groups with the membership
3. New member strategy

4. New fund-raiser
5. New programming
6. Getting more people involved in fund-raising activities
7. Security

If you want to work with the board, or on the board, tell me and I'll find something for you that matches your desires. We need your help.

I have lots of quotes on what a profit-making company should do to make a profit, such as the following:

From Ralph Parilla: "Pay for results. Pay for performance, but don't pay for effort."

From Michael Eisner: "Most people succeed because they work harder than anyone else."

"Progress always involves risk. You can't steal second base and keep your foot on first." (Anon)

From Josh Billings: "Consider the usefulness of the postage stamp; its usefulness consists in the ability to stick to one thing until it gets there.

From Lewis Cass: "People may doubt what you say, but they will believe what you do."

The bottom line is that Congregation Beth Jacob is what you make of it. This place has great rabbis, a great staff, and a wonderful group of members, many whom I consider good friends. I have caught the vision of this synagogue, and I trust that you have too. But you never bet on a vision, you bet on people. For a synagogue, people are everything, and much of the work must be done by volunteers. Yet it is hard to manage people who volunteer because they are not motivated by money but by love. I would prefer to have you work for this shul out of love, but I will allow you to work for the shul and criticize it too. What I can't accept is to let you criticize without working on the solution, for then you are part of the problem and not part of the solution. We have room for you in the shul, regardless of your level of observance, your sex, or your marital status. If you are here for lunch, then at least you have a strong interest in what we are doing. I want your help, I need your help, and with your help there is no limit to what we can accomplish.

January 10

As I begin my second term as your president, I have the high privilege to announce the men of the year and the women of the year. In 2003, there were many people who worked hard for this shul, and we shall honor most of them at the installation lunch right after Kiddush this morning. However, the few I will honor now from the pulpit have all devoted enormous time, energy, and passion to the jobs they undertook last year. Each of them follows a statement by Jim Bleech that "excuses and results are mutually exclusive." These people produce results. I will do the women first.

The women of the year come in three. They worked as a team, and they created from scratch the most successful nonreligious fund-raiser in the history of the synagogue. They worked on this project almost full time for the better part of a year. They put together a huge team at this synagogue that worked efficiently under their direction. These ladies divided the effort as one would run a successful company. The CEO was in charge of strategy and sales, the second lady took on all administrative activities, and the third lady ran operations. They showed us what teamwork is all about and that this shul is capable of greatness. You know what I am talking about—it was the first ever Southeast Kosher Festival and the women of the year are—Roberta Scher, Judy Lipis, and Lynne Rabinowitz. Would you, ladies, please come up to the pulpit to receive your plaques.

Turning to the men of the year, they did not work on a single project together, but each in turn has showed tremendous leadership in keeping this shul financially sound. The first man of the year knows more about the financial condition of the shul than any other lay leader. He has served as the acting executive director of BJ gratis, he was vice president of finance for at least six years and worried about meeting the payroll, week after week, year after year, so you could enjoy the benefits of Beth Jacob without any worry. He worried for you, and my only regret is that he has retired from active board membership this year. The first man of the year is Ira Bodker.

The second man of the year is my predecessor Arnie Schneider. Arnie continues to be almost as active as past president as when he was president. He takes care of e-mail messages, not an insignificant job; he attends virtually all board meetings. He serves as my advisor, he worked hard on the annual directory to make it successful, and he does many other significant fund-raising projects without being asked because he can do them, and he always gets the job done.

Please come up to the pulpit for your plaques, the men of the year—Ira Bodker and Arnie Schneider.

Each of these people are real winners. They are eagles who had vision, commitment, and the ability to execute. They are what H. Ross Perot said, "Eagles don't flock—you have to find them one at a time."

January 17

Here are my quotes for today:

From Joe Pyne: "People will forget what you say; people will even forget what you did, but people will never forget how you made them feel."

From Somerset Maugham: "It's a funny thing about life. If you refuse to accept anything but the best, you often get it."

From Tom Lehrer: "I know that there are people in this world who do not love their fellow man, and I hate people like that."

January 24

Given two bar mitzvahs, I present to you quotes on children and men:

From Harold S. Hulbert: "Children need love, especially when they do not deserve it."

From Hodding Carter: "There are only two lasting bequests we can hope to give our children. One of these is roots; the other is wings."

From William James: "The greatest revolution of our generation is the discovery that human beings, by changing the inner attitudes of their minds can change the outer aspects of their lives."

From George Kirkpatrick: "God gave man two ends—one to sit on and one to think with. Ever since then man's success or failure has been dependent on the one he used the most."

January 31

With the Super Bowl on tomorrow, here are a couple of football quotes:

From Joe Paterno, football coach of Penn State University: "You need to play with supreme confidence; otherwise you will lose again; and then losing becomes a habit."

From Vince Lombardi, football coach of the Green Bay Packers: "The difference between a successful person and others is not a lack of strength, not a lack of knowledge, but rather a lack of will."

Columnist George Will said, "Football combines two of the worst things in American life. It is violence punctuated by committee meetings."

Finally, the comedian, Joe E. Lewis, said, "Show me a man with both feet on the ground and I'll show you a man who can't get his pants on."

February 14

Today I give you three F-words: fanatic, food, and fool.

Winston Churchill said, "A fanatic is one who can't change his mind and won't change the subject."

For food, Joseph Kern said this pun, "Obesity is really widespread." And Robert Quillen said, "Another good reducing exercise consists in placing both hands against the table edge and pushing away."

Finally, Elbert Hubbard said, "Every man is a complete fool for at least five minutes every day; wisdom consists of not exceeding the limit."

February 21

In honor of the Kosher Festival, here are my quotes:

From Andy Rooney: "The biggest seller is cookbooks and the second is diet books—how not to eat what you've just learned how to cook."

From Jack Sharkey: "Jack Sprat could eat no fat, his wife could eat no lean. A real sweet pair of neurotics."

From Joe E. Lewis: "I went on a diet, swore off drinking and heavy eating, and in fourteen days I lost two weeks."

February 28

My quotes for today are in keeping with the Southeast Kosher Festival's success and the Purim Parade tomorrow:

From Frank Lloyd Wright: "The thing always happens that you really believe in; and the belief in the thing makes it happen."

From Henry Ford: "Think you can, think you can't; either way you will be right."

From Joey Adams: "Rockefeller once explained the secret of his success. 'Get up early, work late, and strike oil.'"

March 6

The rumor on the street is that my acting in the Purim Seudah dinner tomorrow night is up for an Oscar. Don't miss this original movie the Swindling Swine. It is hilarious.

In light of our movie tomorrow, tell me the movies these three famous quotes come from:

"Then close your eyes and tap your heels together three times. And think to yourself, 'There's no place like home.'"
—Dorothy (Judy Garland), The Wizard of Oz

"Louis, I think this is the beginning of a beautiful friendship"
—Rick (Humphrey Bogart), Casablanca

"Come on in, and try not to ruin everything by being you."
—Carol (Helen Hunt), As Good As it Gets

March 13

In the past three weeks, we have completed three major activities—the Kosher Festival, the Purim Festival, and the Purim Seudah. Many of you responded to my e-mail to evaluate the Kosher Festival. Thank you for doing it. I will pass it on to our committee for next year. If you attended the Purim Festival or the Purim Seudah, I would also like to have your evaluation of them. Please send me a confidential e-mail. I hope to conduct an assessment of each of our major events to provide feedback to those who worked on them and for next year's committee.

Since everyone who worked on these events needs praise, here are my quotes on praise:

"Most of us can run pretty well all day on one compliment."

From Robert Henley: "A man [or woman] doesn't live by bread alone. They need buttering up once in a while."

From John F. Kennedy: "I think this is the most extraordinary collection of talent, of human knowledge, that has ever been gathered at the White House—with the possible exception of when Thomas Jefferson dined alone."

March 19

Diane Frolov and Andrew Schneider have said, "One person can have a profound effect on another. And two people . . . well, two people can work miracles." Well, there are more than two working miracles in this shul. This Kiddush honors all those who volunteered and worked for this shul. Cicero once said, "Gratitude is not only the greatest of virtues, but the parent of all others." You have our gratitude. Today's Kiddush comes courtesy of your volunteer Kiddush committee, another group that works hard unselfishly and deserves our gratitude. If you have worked as a volunteer on the Southeast Kosher Festival, the Purim Festival, the Purim Seudah, or the Kiddush committee, please stand now so we can honor all of you. Thank you.

Each year the federation asks Jewish organizations in Atlanta to select a Woman of Achievement, a woman who has made an outstanding contribution to their organization and deserves recognition by the wider Jewish community. After serious consideration of the many, many women who could be recognized for their efforts at this synagogue, we have selected Lois Held for this recognition. She is an outstanding choice, and it is well deserved.

I know that all of you work for this shul out of your love for it, and we love you back for it. As David Viscott has said, "To love and be loved is to feel the sun from both sides."

March 27

This shul strives for leadership, so here are my quotes for today:

From the desk of Ted Turner: "Either lead, follow or get out of the way."

From Dale Carnegie: "There is only one way under high Heaven to get anybody to do anything. And that is by making the other person want to do it. Remember, there is no other way."

From Groucho Marx: "Only one man in a thousand is a leader of men—the other 999 follow women."

April 3

Today, our rabbi will present the beginning of the vision he has for this shul. In that light, here is my quote on vision:

From Peter Drucker: "Leadership is not magnetic personality—that can just as well be a glib tongue. It is not 'making friends and influencing people'—that is flattery. Leadership is lifting a person's vision to higher sights, the raising of a person's performance to a higher standard, the building of a personality beyond its normal limitations."

I believe that's what parents should do for their children, what teachers should do for their students, and what rabbis should do for their congregation.

April 7: Pesach

At this time when we celebrate our freedom, here are a few quotes about freedom:

From Archibald MacLeish: "Freedom is the right to choose: the right to create for yourself the alternative of choice."

From Adlai Stevenson: "A free society is one where it is safe to be unpopular."

From Virginia Woolf: "To enjoy freedom we have to control ourselves."

From Marshall Lumsden: "At no time is freedom of speech more precious than when a man hits his thumb with a hammer."

April 8: Pesach

At this time when we celebrate Pesach, and the focus is on teaching children the story of our freedom, here are a few quotes about children:

From John Wilmot: "Before I got married I had six theories about bringing up children; now I have six children and no theories."

From Peter de Vries: "The value of marriage is not that adults produce children, but that children produce adults."

From Hodding Carter: "There are only two lasting bequests we can hope to give our children. One of these is roots; the other wings."

April 10

Following the theme of our rabbi toward lofty dreams, here are a few quotes about the power of positive thinking:

From Tyron Edwards on the power of thought: "Thoughts lead on to purpose; purpose goes forth in action; actions form habits; habits decide character; and character fixes our destiny."

From Frank Hughes on being optimistic: "I will say this about being an optimist; even when things don't turn out well, you are certain they will get better.

From Mike Todd on money: "I've never been poor, only broke. Being poor is a frame of mind. Being broke is a temporary situation."

April 17

Some people have asked me where I get my quotes. I have a large collection of them in books; they are available on the Internet, and sometimes people send them to me. Here are a few great quotes from a book called The Most Brilliant Thoughts of All Time:

From Sir Max Beerbohm, a brilliant English parodist and master of polished prose: "Only mediocrity can be trusted to be always at its best."

From Eleanor Roosevelt: "No one can make you feel inferior without your consent."

From Bernard Bailey, an English economist who died in 1902: "When science discovers the center of the universe, a lot of people will be disappointed to find they are not it."

May 8

Since tomorrow is Mother's Day, I thought I would provide a few quotes about mothers:

I know I told you this quote before, but it is worth repeating from Henry Ward Beecher: "The most important thing a father can do for his children is to love their mother."

Here is a poem from Strickland Gillilan called "Richer Than Gold":

"You may have tangible wealth untold;
Caskets of jewels and coffers of gold;
Richer than I you can never be—
I had a mother who read to me."

From Buddy Hackett: "My mother's menu consisted of two choices: take it or leave it."

May 15

With the school year ending soon, here are two quotes about education:

For all of us as students, there is this quote from Wilson Mizner: "I respect faith, but doubt gets you an education."

For all the teachers, there is this quote from Henry Adams: "A teacher affects eternity; he or she can never tell where his or her influence stops."

And finally, for all of us from Fred Allen: "I always have trouble remembering three things: faces, names and I can't remember what the third thing is."

May 26: Shavuos

Here are two quotes for Shavous:

From Albert Gordon: "Without the Torah the Jew is a body without a soul."

From Hillel: "The more Torah, the more life. The more study, the more wisdom. The more counsel, the more discernment. The more charity, the more peace." Mishna: Abot, 2.7

May 28

Here are some thoughts on the business of money and being rich:

From Henrik Ibsen: "Money may be the husk of many things, but not the kernel. It brings you food, but not appetite; medicine, but not health; acquaintances, but not friends; servants but not faithfulness; days of joy but not peace or happiness."

From William Boetcker: "If you want to know how rich you really are, find out what would be left of you tomorrow if you should lose every dollar you own today."

From Jules Renard: "I finally know what distinguishes man from the other beasts: financial worries."

June 5

Here are six statements about the Business of Life from J. Ogden Armour. He inherited his family's Armour meat-packing business in 1901.

Warned by his father not to let wealth ruin him, he turned the company into a conglomerate with more than three thousand products:

1. Good men are not cheap.
2. Capital can do nothing without the brains to direct it.
3. No general can fight his battles alone. He must depend upon his lieutenants, and his success depends upon his ability to secure the right man for the right place.
4. There is no such thing as luck.
5. Most men talk too much. Much of my success has been due to keeping my mouth shut.
6. The young man who wants to marry happily should pick out a good mother and marry one of her daughters—anyone will do.

June 12

This Sunday night at 8:00 p.m., Rabbi Ilan will make a special presentation to our board of trustees on the vision he has for our synagogue. If you would like to hear this presentation, you are invited to attend as an observer. I expect this presentation to help the board define its strategy for the future.

Regarding vision, here are a few quotes about living up to your vision:

From Watterson Lowe: "Nobody grows old by merely living a number of years. People grow old by deserting their ideals. Years wrinkle the face, but to give up enthusiasm wrinkles the soul. Worry, doubt, self-interest, fear, despair—these are the long, long years that bow the head and turn the growing spirit back to dust."

From Sir Richard Tangye: "During a very busy life I have often been asked, 'How did you manage to do it all?' The answer is very simple: It is because I did everything promptly."

From George W. Blount: "If you have something to do that is worthwhile doing, don't talk about it, but do it. After you have done it, your friends and enemies will talk about it."

June 19

In addition to those sponsoring Kiddush that the rabbi announced, the congregation is also sponsoring Kiddush today in honor of the rabbi's fiftieth Hebrew birthday, which will occur June 27 when the rabbi will be out of town celebrating sheva brachos on the occasion of his daughter's wedding. Mazel Tov.

In honor of the rabbi's future milestone, I offer you the following quotes:

From Glenn Clark: "If you wish to travel and fast, travel light. Take off all your envies, jealousies, unforgiveness, selfishness and fears."

From Bruce Barton: "If you expect perfection from people, your whole life is a series of disappointments, grumblings and complaints. If, on the contrary, you pitch your expectations low, taking folks as the inefficient creatures which they are, you are frequently surprised by having them perform better than you had hoped."

And finally, a most appropriate remark from Thomas Jefferson: "Speeches that are measured by the hour will die with the hour."

July 3

For our bar mitzvah today, here are my quotes:

From Lady Bird Johnson: "Children are likely to live up to what you believe of them."

From Mordecai Kaplan: "An Optimist is one who believes that this is the best of all possible worlds, and a pessimist is one who is afraid that the optimist is right. The problem is not whether it is best or worst, but how to go about making it better."

From Nicholas Murray Butler: "The world can be divided into 3 groups: those who make things happen, those who watch things happen, and those who wonder what happened."

July 10

I want you to know that the financial situation at our synagogue is deteriorating. Your board and your staff are working on a multipart solution. While I do not have a definitive plan today, I hope to lay out a plan for you shortly. With that in mind, here are my quotes for today:

From Dinah Shore: "There are no hopeless situations—only people who are hopeless about them."

Next: "There are too many people praying for mountains of difficulty to be removed, when what they really need is courage to climb them."

And finally, there is the story of a rabbi who got up one Shabbos and announced to his congregation: "I have good news and bad news. The good news is—we have enough money to pay for our new building program. The bad news is, it's still out there in your pockets."

July 17

Please take note of the beautiful rotunda that will shortly display the plaques for those paid up on their rededication fund pledge. Please get in touch with the office to proofread your inscription so we can put up your plaque with the others plaques. I think you will be impressed with the results.

Here are a few famous quotes from Mahatma Gandhi:

First: "There is more to life than simply increasing its speed."

Second: "Live as if you were to die tomorrow. Learn as if you were to live forever."

Last: "An eye for eye only ends up making the whole world blind."

July 24

Please see Avraham about any of the fund-raisers you want to help.

In line with that theme, here are seven quotes for today:

The first is from Rabbi Ilan Feldman: "Raising money for a shul is not just about supporting your synagogue; it is about sanctifying God's name. Without money it will be just a little bit harder."

From Alexander Pope: "He who serves his brother best gets nearer God than all the rest."

From Eleanor Roosevelt: "If I were asked what is the best thing we can expect in life, I would say—the privilege of being useful."

George Washington Carver: "It is not the cut of a man's coat, not the manner of his dress. It's service that measures success."

From Stevie Wonder: "In my career, I have learned that giving of your services for free gives you a good return on your investment, not just financially but morally. It supplements my personal integrity."

From Sir Wilfred Grenfell: "The service we render to others is really the rent we pay for our room on this earth."

"There are Ten rules for getting rid of the blues: Go out and do something nice for someone else; then repeat it nine times."—Author Unkown

July 31

I don't want to be serious today; it's summer, it's vacation time. It's time to play. Here are some of the best quips I know:

From John Kirk Nelson: "More and more these days I find myself pondering on how to reconcile my net income with my gross habits."

Hobart Brown: "Money doesn't always bring happiness. People with ten million dollars are no happier than people with nine million dollars."

From Gloria Swanson (on looking at her passport photo): "If I looked like this, I need the trip."

Charles M. Schulz (from Peanuts): "I have a new philosophy. I'm only going to dread one day at a time."

From Groucho Marx: "I never forget a face, but in your case I'll make an exception."

August 7

The death of Henry Hirsch this past week brings me up short, for I am his age, and he was one of the very best we had. He wasn't a chip off the old block; he was the block itself. Then today, we have a beautiful bar mitzvah, a real occasion to celebrate.

On behalf of all of us who know not what life brings from day to day, here are my quotes for you:

From Baal Shem Tov: "The world is new to us every morning—this is God's gift, and every person should believe he is reborn every day."

Adlai Stevenson: "It is not the years in your life but the life in your years that counts."

From Robert Frost: "In three words I can sum up everything I've learned about life. It goes on."

From Joe E. Lewis: "You only live once, but if you work it right, once is enough."

August 14

My family will be going on vacation soon, so family is on my mind. Here are my quotes for today:

From Walter M. Schirra Sr. (the father of one of our astronauts): "You don't raise heroes; you raise sons. And if you treat them like sons, they'll turn out to be heroes, even if it's just in your own eyes."

From Harry S. Truman: "I have found that the best way to give advice to your children is to find out what they want and then advise them to do it."

How many times, in frustration with your child, have you said, "When you grow up I hope you have a child just like you, so you'll know what I'm going through."

September 3

There will be a memorial service tomorrow morning at 10:00 a.m. at Young Israel to say good-bye to Rabbi Larry Meltzer, who will be buried in Israel. Larry was a close friend of mine for many years, as is his wife, Sandy. My daughter grew up with his daughter, and Rabbi Meltzer taught my children as a member of the faculty at the Hebrew Academy. I, for one, will miss his sweet disposition, his love of life, his brilliance, and his ability to be an observant Jew without ever making a judgment of anyone else.

We often complain about petty things in life, and when we lose a friend like this, I am comforted by the following from the works of Max Ehrmann:

"Go placidly amid the noise and the haste, and remember what peace there is in silence. As far as possible without surrender, be on good terms with all persons. Be yourself. Take kindly the counsel of the years, gracefully surrendering the things of youth. Be gentle with yourself. You are a child of the universe, no less than the trees and the stars; you have a right to be here. And whether or not it is clear to you, no doubt the universe is unfolding as it should. Therefore, be at peace with God, whatever you conceive Him to be, and whatever your labors and aspirations, in the noisy confusion of life keep peace with your soul. With all its sham, drudgery and broken dreams, it is still a beautiful world."

September 10

I have one quote today. It comes from a movie based on a famous book called The Count of Monte Cristo. A priest in prison, who is dying in his cell, tells Edmund Dantes, the hero of the book, who was falsely thrown in prison, "This is your final lesson, do not seek vengeance, for God said, 'Vengeance is mine.' Dantes then says, 'I don't believe in God.' The priest then says, 'It doesn't matter, God believes in you.'"

September 17: Rosh Hashanah

On behalf of your board of trustees, I wish you and your family a fabulous New Year, full of health, prosperity, and peace. I hope this is your best year ever. A New Year is a time for new beginnings, for taking stock, and setting new goals. I wish you all great success in whatever you do.

Here are a few quotes related to reaching your goals:

From Benjamin Mays: "The tragedy of life doesn't lie in not reaching your goal. The tragedy lies in having no goal to reach."

From Dwight Eisenhower: "We succeed only as we identify in life, or in war, or in anything else, a single overriding objective, and make all other considerations bend to that objective."

And paraphrasing Samuel Butler: "There are two great rules in life, the general and the particular. The general rule is that you can, in the end, reach your goal and get what you want, if only you try. The particular rule is that everyone, more or less, is an exception to the general rule."

September 17

This shul is not short on ideas. What we need is the execution on our ideas, like what Mickey did with the plaques. In that vane, here are a few quotes on getting things done.

Dr. Frank Crane: "The Golden Rule is of no use to you whatever, unless you realize it is your move."

Duguet: "The smallest good deed is better than the grandest good intention."

Hamilton Holt: "Nothing worthwhile comes easily. Half effort does not produce half results. It produces no results. Work, continuous work and hard work, is the only way to accomplish results that last."

September 29

Here are three outstanding quotes:

From Diane von Furstenberg, a famous clothing designer: "My best creation is my children."

From Soren Kierkegaard: "Prayer does not change God, but it changes him who prays."

From Napoleon I: "Riches do not consist in the possession of treasures, but in the use made of them."

September 30: Succos

My quotations come from many sources, but today's quotation was found by my aunt on a box of tea. I have taken a small liberty to make it plural. It was written by Joseph Newton, and it begins as follows:

"When is a man or a woman educated? When they can look upon the universe, now lucid and lovely, now dark and terrible, with a sense of their own littleness in the great scheme of things, and yet have faith and courage. When they know how to make friends and keep them, and above all, when they can keep friends with themselves. People are educated when they can be happy alone and high-minded amid the drudgeries of life; when they can look into a wayside puddle and see something besides mud, and into the face of the most forlorn mortal and see something divine; when they know how to live, how to love, how to hope, how to pray . . . and have in their heart a bit of a song."

October 1: Succos

Normally, I will only thank the young man who finishes the davening. However, the Chazans, our Chazanim this new year, who have sung for us from Rosh Hashanah to Yom Kippur and now for Succos, have been nothing short of spectacular. We have heard beautiful voices, a huge variety of tunes and a passion from each one of them to represent us to Hashem above. We have even had a small choir that in itself was inspiring. But more than anything, each individually has given his very best, and together they have given us a spirituality that is rarely matched elsewhere. They have all sung with the words from Henini, the Chazan's prayer before Mussaf on Rosh Hashanah: "Accept my prayer as if I were entirely qualified and well-pleasing to my fellow men." And they were. "Convey my prayer before Thy glorious throne and present it to Thee in the name of all the upright and honest men and women." And they did. I don't want to mention them by name, but I want to thank them all for making these holidays very, very special, and there is nothing else to say but thank you for sharing your voices and your spirituality with us. Yasher Koach.

Here are some quotations related to music and singing:

From Thomas Carlyle: "Music is well said to be the speech of angels; in fact, nothing among the utterances allowed to man is felt to be so divine. It brings us near to the infinite."

There is a lovely saying that applies to each of our Chazanim: "The song is ended but the melody lingers on."

But perhaps the most famous singing quote is this: "It ain't over till the fat lady sings." And she won't be singing here anytime soon.

October 8: Simchat Torah

Now Simchat Torah is a day for rejoicing, so here are quotations about happiness:

From Charles "Tremendous" Jones: "If you can't be happy where you are, it's a cinch you can't be happy where you ain't."

Contemplate this: "Just think how happy you would be if you lost everything you have right now—and then got it back again."

From Henry Miller: "I have no money, no resources, no hopes. I am the happiest man alive."

October 9

I am going to stick with a single person for my quotations, and I begin with one of the very best, Dorothy Parker, who happens to be Jewish.

She had a sharp tongue and a very quick wit. You will see how clever she is by listening to these quotations:

You can't teach an old dogma new tricks.
Brevity is the soul of lingerie.
The only "ism" Hollywood believes in is plagiarism
Oh, life is a glorious cycle of song,
A medley of extemporanea;
And love is a thing that can never go wrong;
And I am Marie of Roumania.

October 23

With the theme of courage in mind, here are my quotes:

From Andrew Jackson: "One man with courage makes a majority."

From George Tilton: "Success is never final and failure never fatal. It's courage that counts."

The rabbi and I both have the courage to ask you, "What are we doing right for you and what could we be doing better for you?" Please give us an answer.

October 30

With the election a few days away, here are clever political quotes:

From the Democrat Adlai Stevenson in 1952: "If the Republicans stop telling lies about us, we will stop telling the truth about them."

From Mark Twain: "Suppose you were an idiot. And suppose you were a member of Congress. But, I repeat myself."

From a Johnny Carson 1991 monologue: "Democracy is buying a big house you can't afford, with money you don't have, to impress people you wish were dead. And, unlike communism, democracy does not mean having just one ineffective political party; it means having two ineffective political parties. Democracy is welcoming people from other lands, and giving them something to hold onto—usually a mop or a leaf blower. It means that with proper timing and scrupulous bookkeeping, anyone can die owing the government a huge amount of money. Democracy means free television, not good television, but free. And finally, democracy is the eagle on the back of a dollar bill, with 13 arrows in one claw, 13 leaves on a branch, 13 tail feathers, and 13 stars over its head—this signifies that when the white man came to this country, it was bad luck for the Indians, bad luck for the trees, bad luck for the wildlife, and lights out for the American eagle."

November 6

Today's quotations come from sports. Here they are:

From Supreme Court Justice Earl Warren: "I always turn to the sports page first. The sports page records people's accomplishments; the front page nothing but man's failures."

From Vince Lombardi (Green Bay Packers): "The difference between a successful person and others is not a lack of strength, not a lack of knowledge, but rather a lack of will."

From Bobby Knight (University of Indiana): "The will to succeed is important, but what's even more important is the will to prepare."

From Michael Jordan (basketball star): "I've always believed that if you put in the work, the results will come. I don't do things half-heartedly. Because I know if I do, then I can expect half-hearted results."

November 13

As I look back on my nearly two years as president of this shul, I can only remark that this is the quietest shul in America, that this sanctuary is very inspiring, and our facility overall is very impressive for us and for our visitors, who admire it simchas after simchas. We have much to be proud of—our past, our present, and our future.

That leads me to the quotes for the future:

From Charles Kettering: "My interest in the future is because I expect to spend the rest of my life there."

From George Bernard Shaw: "The reasonable man adapts himself to the world; the unreasonable man persists to adapt the world to himself. Therefore all progress depends on the unreasonable man."

From Robert F. Kennedy: "Some people see things as they are and say why. I dream things that never were and say why not?"

From Hendrik Willem van Loon: "High up in the North in the land called Svithjod, there stands a rock. It is 100 miles high and 100 miles wide. Once every thousand years a little bird comes to this rock to sharpen its beak. When the rock has thus been worn away, then a single day of eternity will have gone by."

November 20

This past Thursday night, your board passed the budget for 2005. It only can be balanced if the many fund-raising programs we have planned are all successful. Fortunately, your nominations committee has put together a terrific set of officers for next year and has added several new members that are excited about serving this synagogue. I believe we have the will to succeed beyond our expectations, and I think this shul will be in excellent hands for the coming year.

With that in mind, I offer you these thoughts about our board of trustees from Pirkei Avos:

Rabban Gamliel said: "All who exert themselves for the community should exert themselves for the sake of Heaven." I believe your board has no other motive.

Shammai says: "Say little and do much." These five little words say so much. Your board strives for this, and yet we can do better.

And finally from Simeon the Just: "It is not up to you to complete the task, yet you are not free to withdraw from it." In this regard, no one person needs to do it all, not even your board; rather all of us are obligated to make our contribution to the full extent of our abilities.

December 4

Two weeks ago, this shul held its first Texas Hold 'Em Poker tournament; it was a huge success. In honor of that occasion, here are quotes on winning from boxing, football, and horse racing:

From H. E. Jansen: "The man who wins may have been counted out several times, but he didn't hear the referee."

From Vince Lombardi: "Winning is not a sometime thing: it's an all the time thing. You don't win once in a while; you don't do the right thing once in a while; you do them right all the time. Winning is a habit. Unfortunately, so is losing."

From Willie Shoemaker, the famous jockey: "There are one hundred and ninety nine ways to beat, but only one way to win; get there first."

By the way, I won the poker tournament and I've got the plaque to prove it. It reads, "Beth Jacob Charity Texas Hold 'Em Champion, 2004." I do intend to make a substantial contribution of my winnings to the shul. And right after that, I'm quitting my job, selling my house, and I'm moving to Las Vegas to become a professional gambler.

December 11

I hope that what I had to say had some impact on you, for I did prepare every time so as not to waste your time. I focused on quotations because they are well said, they are insightful, and they are worth remembering. Quotations gave me great leeway to be funny or serious or neither, drawing on brilliant minds over centuries of thought. I probably gained the most from the process.

For today, I want to give you a short course in human relations that fits nicely with Pirkei Avos, "The Ethics of Our Fathers":

The six most important words: I admit that I was wrong. That's repentance.

The five most important words: You did a great job. That's honoring others.

The four most important words: What do you think? That's promoting unity.

The three most important words: Could you please? That's avoiding power.

The two most important words: Thank you. That's gratitude.

The most important word: We. That's sharing joy.

The least important word: I. That's humility.

December 18

Since I will be on vacation next week, this is my last Shabbos to speak to you as your president. Tomorrow at 11:00 a.m., we will hold our annual congregational meeting, and I will present the State of Our Synagogue and try to answer your questions. Then we will elect a slate of officers and other board members for next year. Please come and speak up.

I will only say that it has been a grand privilege and a high honor to serve you and this wonderful shul. This synagogue will always be very special for me, for it allowed me to grow as a Jew while I played some small part in the mission of this great institution.

As always, I leave you with words of wisdom. These particular quotations have all been hanging on the side of my bookcase for more than a decade:

From Jean Anouilh: "Things are beautiful if you love them."

From Collette: "Be happy. It is a way of being wise."

From William James: "Be not afraid of life. Believe that life is worth living and your belief will help create the fact."

Finally, I want to leave you with a blessing that has been close to me. It is so close that I have been sitting on it for two years. I am talking about the words on the chair I sit on during services. In my mind, it has become my chair; and when someone switched the chair one week to the rabbi's side, I switched it back to my side. That chair has four words on it:

כתבנו בספר חיים טובים

Inscribe us in the book of Good life. May it be a blessing for each of you.